Original title:
Life's Purpose Is Overrated Anyway

Copyright © 2025 Creative Arts Management OÜ
All rights reserved.

Author: Maya Livingston
ISBN HARDBACK: 978-1-80566-125-2
ISBN PAPERBACK: 978-1-80566-420-8

The Subtle Art of Discontent

Chasing dreams like a cat in a tree,
Only to find it's a branch of misery.
I thought I'd soar, but I just trip,
Can someone please grab me a snack to sip?

Each day feels like a game of charades,
Pretending to dance while the world parades.
I raise my glass to the mundane spree,
Here's to the chaos that sets me free!

Emptiness Woven with Hope

Tangled in threads of my swirling mind,
Searching for treasures I can't seem to find.
Like socks in the dryer, they disappear,
Is it hope I'm crafting or just a souvenir?

A blank canvas calls with a mocking grin,
I throw on some paint, but it's all a whim.
Life's a buffet, piled high and wide,
But I'm just here for the dessert to ride!

Embracing the Chaos of Being

Life's a puzzle with missing pieces,
Do I need them all, or just some releases?
I juggle my complaints like a circus act,
Hoping the audience gets some good cracks!

Wandering aimlessly like a lost kite,
Tangled in strings, what a beautiful sight.
I cheer for the chaos, I raise my mug,
To the mess of existence and all its shrug!

Silent Conversations with the Universe

Whispers echo through the twinkling night,
I shout back questions, quite a bold sight.
The stars just chuckle, they don't give clues,
Oh, cosmic buddy, what's with these blues?

I'm chatting with planets, all in a buzz,
They nod at my antics, now that's what 'was'.
In the grand play, do we ever really know,
If the punchlines matter or just the show?

The Language of Simple Moments

A toast to socks that don't quite match,
A dance with crumbs upon the patch.
We laugh at plans that fell apart,
And find the joy in every fart.

With coffee spills and missed alarms,
The chaos brings unmeasured charms.
We chase the dawn without a care,
Embracing life's wild, messy flair.

Shadows of Aimlessness

We trip on thoughts that seem so grand,
Yet linger slow, like grains of sand.
The GPS just leads to snacks,
Our wanderings greet simple hacks.

With every aimless stroll we take,
We find new trails, a piece of cake.
Who needs a map or clear intent?
Life's a jest, it's all content!

The Joys of Just Being

With comfy chairs and lazy days,
We navigate this quirky maze.
Fuzzy socks and pizza dreams,
In silliness, we find our themes.

Why rush the race that has no lane?
We'll hug the couch, embrace the gain.
Our purpose lost, but who can tell?
We dance right past the wishing well.

Moments that Whistle Past

Time winks at us and strolls away,
Like socks found at the end of day.
We juggle thoughts like oranges tossed,
And cheer for all the time we lost.

In a world that calls for goals to chase,
We snicker at the human race.
So here we sit, with snacks to share,
Embracing moments floating in air.

Epiphanies in the Unseen

Sometimes I trip on a sock,
Could this be my calling?
A dance of the mundane,
In chaos, I hear the calling.

Glimpses of wisdom arise,
While I'm searching for snacks,
The universe laughs at me,
Life hides in these little cracks.

Coffee spills, oh what fun,
My fortune in a mug,
Perhaps the truth's in the grind,
Not found in a heartfelt hug.

Lost in a sea of laundry,
I unfurl my grand plan,
The deep meaning I seek,
May just be in my flan.

Freedom Found in Little Things

A tiny bird sings at dawn,
In pajamas, I happily sway.
Chasing thoughts in a lemonade,
The sun seems to smile and play.

Finding joy in dust bunnies,
As I search beneath the bed,
I ponder the wisdom in crumbs,
Or in the shoes I never shed.

Silly dances in the kitchen,
With a spatula as a mic,
In grand schemes I'm not interested,
It's the spice of life I like.

Bubble wrap and silly hats,
Make the drudgery seem light,
In chaos, I find my freedom,
And the silly seems just right.

The Weight of a Thousand Wishes

A wish upon a star tonight,
But I still can't find my keys,
Maybe wishes are just fluff?
Or in a dandelion breeze?

I ponder on epic desires,
While I trip over my cat,
What if happiness is small?
Like a cookie and a nap?

With a mountain of small aims,
A build-up of sweet regret,
Perhaps the weight's just a burp,
Or an unfinished croquet set.

Wishing wells are a blast,
But I'll stick to wishing well,
Trading grand schemes for pizza,
Where every slice's a spell.

Life Without a Script

They say life's a grand performance,
But I can't find the script.
I'm lost between the punchlines,
In improv, I'm fully equipped.

With actors in mismatched socks,
And plot twists that go awry,
We're all fumbling for our cue,
While the scene steals the sky.

My lines come with a hiccup,
As I forget the guidebook,
Yet laughter breaks the silence,
In chaos, we truly look.

So here's to moments unplanned,
To a life where we just wing,
In the absence of a script, my friend,
We become the jester and king.

Unraveled Aspirations

I tied my dreams with a silly string,
But they all fell down, what a funny thing!
A plan so grand, you'd think I'd win,
Instead, I'm lost in my own spin.

I chased careers like a puppy in play,
Only to find I'd rather nap all day.
The ladder I climbed was really just art,
A montage of chaos, a loopy heart.

They say to strive, reach for the stars,
While I binge-watch shows and munch on jars.
With shaky hands, I flutter and flap,
My aspiration turned into a nap.

So here's to chasing whims in a dance,
Trading purpose for a silly chance.
For when you laugh at the things you sought,
You find out joy was the only thought.

The Secret Life of Daydreams

In a world of dreams, I plan my schemes,
But coffee spills drown all my memes!
A knight in armor? Nah, just a chair,
As I sit and ponder, and twirl my hair.

I dreamt of riches, a palace so grand,
But my bank account is merely bland.
With a cat on my lap, I conquer the land,
In my mind's kingdom, it's all so unplanned!

With unicorns dancing in the bright sky,
I scribble my wins with a glittery tie.
Yet reality nudges with a cheeky grin,
"Hey, what about laundry and where have you been?"

So, I sneak back to dreams where I rule,
Riding rainbows while following 'cool.'
In the end, it's fun, not burdens imposed,
Daydreams are treasures; I'm simply disposed.

Knotting Threads of Meaninglessness

I knotted my life with a rogue shoelace,
Tripped on my purpose, fell right on my face!
With tangled thoughts, I spin like a top,
Thinking of reaching but never to stop.

Threads of ambition in colors so bright,
Only to fade with a well-timed bite.
My needle's aim goes as far as my snack,
Sewing confusion, but I'm never on track!

I tried to create a masterpiece here,
But it looks like a jigsaw with pieces unclear.
So I giggle and stitch with a chuckle and glee,
For meaning was just a tangled ol' spree.

Embrace the chaos, the fibers of fun,
We're all just knots, tangled and spun.
With laughter as the thread through which we glide,
Let's dance with absurdity, joy as our guide.

When the Quest Ends in Laughter

I set out on a quest, sword in one hand,
To find what I sought in a far-off land.
But the map I used was all upside down,
And led me right to a lost-and-found town.

I sought wisdom from wise, old owls,
But they hooted back with their silly prowls.
Turns out the treasure was a rubber chicken,
Quacking at wisdom, what a funny mission!

The goalposts moved like a game without score,
And laughter bubbled to the very core.
So I threw out plans, danced on my feet,
With each hearty chuckle, the quest felt complete.

When burdens felt heavy, I'd lean on my jokes,
With friends who laugh, we're the happiest folks.
For every misstep in this odd little dance,
Ends with a giggle, a second chance.

Where Wanderlust Meets Stillness

Chasing dreams with rain-soaked shoes,
Yet here I sit, nursing a snooze.
The world spins fast, I manage slow,
To wander far, or not to go?

Maps unfolded, but crumbs insist,
I'm missing out on the toast I've dissed.
Adventure calls, but who needs thrills?
I'm stuck inside, counting my bills.

Reflections in a Dusty Mirror

I look and see a face I know,
But who's this guest, stealing the show?
With every wrinkle, stories bloom,
Though I still can't find the vacuum's room.

Alas, in pursuit of what's profound,
I find my socks, scattered around.
Pick my battles? Or just stand still?
Where's the manual to this old thrill?

The Price of Expectation

I planned a feast, but burnt the bread,
So I'll feast on thoughts instead.
Expectations high, but snacks went low,
A juggling act with a pizza dough.

In search of gold in a pile of sand,
My dreams grow tired; they need a hand.
But laughter's gold, so let's not fret,
I'll eat my crumbs with gusto yet!

A Story Written in Silence

In the quiet moments, I scribble lines,
Between the dishes and grapevine twines.
A novel awaits, but words don't flow,
So I write a blog on my cat's new bow.

In silence, I plot a silly joke,
About a bard who forgot his cloak.
So while the world ponders fate's design,
I'll tackle laundry and sip some wine.

The Weight of Tomorrow's Dreams

I planned to climb the tallest hill,
But tripped on dreams and lost my will.
Chasing feathers in the breeze,
Turns out I'm allergic to trees.

I pondered life, a grand design,
But ketchup on my fries felt fine.
So why chase clouds like they're a prize?
I'll stick to pizza 'til I rise.

Chasing Shadows in a Blurry Mirror

I stared hard at my blurry face,
It winked back, what a funny place!
Is that my future? Just a smudge,
Or did I eat too much fudge?

I chase my shadow, it runs fast,
Silly me, I'm stuck in the past.
With every step, it fades away,
Maybe I'll nap instead, hooray!

Embracing the Art of Wandering

I wanted a map to find my way,
But got distracted by a café.
With pastries calling out my name,
Who needs a path when there's good aim?

I wandered aimlessly all night,
Found a donut shop, what a delight!
If wandering is truly an art,
I'm the Picasso of the heart.

When the Stars Lose Their Meaning

I gazed at stars from my backyard,
To find their meaning seemed quite hard.
They twinkled down, in cosmic jest,
'We're just shiny rocks, take a rest!'

Counted them once, lost track of ten,
And spilt my soda; counts again!
With each sip, I laughed at fate,
Who knew confusion could taste so great?

The Subtle Power of Disillusionment

Chasing dreams that drift away,
I tripped over my own cliché.
Every lesson learned, they say,
Is just a game of hide and play.

With every goal I aim to miss,
I find my peace in mortal bliss.
Turns out the chase is quite absurd,
Like fishing without a single word.

Laughing at Life's Heavy Questions

Why am I here, what's the score?
My couch and snacks keep wanting more.
I ponder deep while sipping tea,
And laugh at what's supposed to be.

Questions float like bubbles high,
Pop! There goes the 'whys' and 'byes'.
Embrace the wobbly, swirling jest,
While peanut butter spreads its best.

The Unfolding of Simple Joys

A woeful soup can warm the heart,
But only if you know your art.
I find my joy in everyday sights,
Like socks that don't match on lazy nights.

Rainy days and muddy shoes,
Become the canvas for my muse.
Chuckling at the little things,
Like when my dog runs off with strings.

Treading Water in a Sea of Significance

I'm treading lightly on this pond,
Where meaning fades and thoughts respond.
Swim with the fish that laugh and play,
And watch the drama float away.

With every splash of quirky thought,
I wear the antics that I've sought.
So here I float, no need to dive,
In shallow waters, I feel alive.

A Canvas Without an Artist

Colors splattered everywhere,
A masterpiece of mess,
The paintbrush took a holiday,
Inventing chaos, I confess.

Who needs a grand design,
When splashes make a scene?
A canvas left untroubled,
Is where we find the green.

The Beauty of Aimless Journeys

Maps are overrated, who needs a guide?
Just hop in the car, forget the pride.
Each turn is a surprise, laughter's the goal,
With snacks in the back, and no sense of control.

Wherever we end up, that's just fine,
Bars and diners with neon signs.
We'll find joy in the wrong turns we make,
Life's like a journey, a piece of cake!

Echoes in a Void of Expectations

Expectations ring a bell, loud and clear,
But I've left them behind; they're not welcome here.
I hum a tune, with no tempo in sight,
Dancing to echoes of wrong and right.

A void with more laughter than thought in my head,
Is a place where the free spirits tread.
No need for a roadmap, no worries today,
Just enjoy the ride, come what may!

Dancing in the Absence of Direction

With no steps to follow, I sway and spin,
A jig without logic, let the fun begin!
My feet do a tango with walls of despair,
Each shuffle's a giggle, not a worry or care.

In circles I wander, with drinks in our hands,
Who needs a plan when joy understands?
Let's dance like no one is watching us here,
In a world where confusion brings nothing but cheer!

Tides of Transformation

Waves roll in, just to roll out,
Splashing hopes like seeds of doubt.
Fish swimming by with no great plan,
Smiling wide, as if they can.

Seagulls squawk without a care,
Laughing at dreams that float inair.
The ocean's depth, a splashy jest,
Reminds us all—just take a rest.

Crabs scuttle sideways, no straight path,
Chasing shadows, missing math.
Sandcastles crumble, no one's alarmed,
Building worries, forever charmed.

Jellyfish dance, though it seems absurd,
Drifting along with thoughts unheard.
So who needs a map, or golden rules?
Just wave hello—and swim, you fools!

Musings Under a Starlit Sky

Stars twinkle like tipsy sprites,
Falling down in silly flights.
What's the point of mapping fate?
Just grab a snack and celebrate!

Clouds drift by like thoughts unplanned,
Chasing dreams with popcorn in hand.
Wishing upon a comet's tail,
Asking questions that never scale.

The moon just grins, a cheeky glow,
Whispering truths we'll never know.
Underneath this cosmic show,
Who needs purpose? Just let it flow!

So dance along the Milky Way,
With giggles, and make a grand bouquet.
Starry nights don't hold a truth,
Just silly thoughts that spark our youth!

The Absurdity of Life's Ladder

Climbing up rickety heights,
Stepping on dreams and silly sights.
Ladders wobble, hearts might race,
But where's the prize in this mad chase?

Cats curl up, on each warm rung,
Taking naps while we feel strung.
With every slip, there's laughter loud,
As purpose gets lost in the crowd.

People climb with maps in hand,
While kittens nap on shifting sand.
With every rung, they reach in vain,
In this circus, they're just insane.

So let's embrace this silly plight,
Forget the top, and take a bite.
Just slide down, and enjoy the ride,
Absurdity is best when amplified!

Embracing the Unremarked Journey

Trails unmarked lead to nowhere great,
Frogs sing songs of a cheeky fate.
Hopping along without a care,
Worry melts like summer air.

Turtles stroll with no set aim,
Finding joy in the silliest game.
Each pebble holds a whimsical tale,
While ants march in a quirky trail.

Life's just a twist, a playful jest,
Like wearing shoes on the wrong foot, best.
To wander off the beaten track,
Is to discover—no need to pack.

So let's embrace each silly turn,
With laughter bright and hearts that burn.
In journeys unremarked, we find the glee,
And dance with joy, wild and free!

The Illusion of a Grand Design

Plans are made with careful thought,
Yet chaos laughs, they come to naught.
Dreams are big, but dogs prefer,
Chasing tails; that's life's grand spur.

Stars won't always align, my friend,
Sometimes they play a twisted blend.
Life's sketchy plans? A doodled mess,
Scribbles on napkins, no less, no less!

Just when you think you've got it right,
A squirrel darts left—oh, what a sight!
Philosophers ponder on a whim,
While we just laugh and sing a hymn.

So raise a glass to all the flops,
To misadventures and funny hops.
In the end, what matters most,
Are the laughs we share, let's make a toast!

Breathing in Imperfect Moments

Sipped my coffee with a grin,
It spilled, but I let the day begin.
A toast to crumbs and missing keys,
Embrace the chaos, if you please.

In tangled sheets, I wake too late,
I laugh out loud; who needs a fate?
Cutting corners, losing track,
Find joy in things we now call 'crack'.

The sun shines bright on dusty roads,
But who needs grams when laughter's loads?
In the mean time, grab a snack,
And let the world be out of whack.

Let's celebrate that fuzzy vibe,
A messy truth that we prescribe.
In every flaw, the charm unfolds,
Uneven paths are the best of gold.

Crumpled Maps of Forgotten Destinations

Folded maps like dreams, they lay,
In drawers deep where they don't play.
Who needs a plan for where to roam?
I'll drive in circles, call it home.

The GPS says next right turn,
I go the left; oh! Watch it burn!
Adventures bloom when lost we feel,
Underlined in stains, surreal.

Travelers laughing at my plight,
"Map? What map?" I say, delight.
Eating lunch atop a car,
With crumpled dreams, we've come so far.

In every wrong and shady place,
Lies laughter's echo, joy in grace.
So let's embrace the road not taken,
In potholes deep, our hearts awaken.

Reflections on a Silent Path

I walk a path where silence reigns,
In quiet moments, laughter gains.
I trip on thoughts that seem so profound,
Only to find they're silly, unbound.

The trees just shrug, the leaves all cheer,
Life's curious quirks, they bring good cheer.
I gaze into the pond's still face,
A tadpole whispers, "What a race!"

Bumping into wisdom's door,
"That's not my name," it says, I pour.
With giggles echoing on the breeze,
I chase the echoes, do as I please.

So here's to paths both loud and mute,
Embracing whims, that's the route!
In every pause, a chuckle lies,
Beneath the sun, in both our eyes.

Meditations on Mediocrity

In the land of average dreams,
We sip our coffee with no themes.
Waking up at half past ten,
Who needs goals? Let's sleep again.

Chasing socks and missing keys,
Life's a puzzle, just a breeze.
We aim for gold, but get a bronze,
Meditating on our lazy con.

Finding joy in sandwich spreads,
While others strive for lofty threads.
Counting bites instead of wins,
In this game, we're all just twins.

So here we sit, with smiles wide,
Content to let the world just glide.
In mediocrity, we shall bask,
No need for dreams, just throw a snack.

A Symphony of Quiet Thoughts

In the hall of echoes soft and neat,
Resides a tune, a skipping beat.
Pajamas on, the world goes by,
We hum along, no need to try.

A symphony of bedhead peaks,
Of cozy socks, and silent squeaks.
Our instruments are chips and dips,
We play the score of lazy quips.

The orchestra of mundane chores,
Conducted by the call of snores.
With every yawn, a note we play,
In our lullabies, we drift away.

So join the dance of slow-paced fun,
Where time is lost, but joy's not done.
In quiet thoughts, we find our voice,
No grand career, but still, rejoice.

The Color of Contentment

In shades of beige and muted grey,
We paint our moments, soft display.
Dancing in socks with no one near,
Contentment lives in kitsch so dear.

A burst of laughter in the sink,
Cleaning dishes, what do we think?
Each splash a joy, each suds a cheer,
Life's more fun when it's sincere.

We'd rather munch on popcorn snacks,
Than climb high walls or face attacks.
Here's to the moments, oh so bland,
In everyday, we make our stand.

So raise a glass of fizzy drink,
To colors bright, and those we wink.
In simple joys, we find our hue,
In lack of frenzy, life feels new.

Wandering Without a Compass

Lost between the couch and fridge,
Adventure calls, just a tiny bridge.
With a remote in hand, we roam,
Exploring dimensions of our home.

The winding path to snacks galore,
Like Vikings trekked on distant shore.
But what's the treasure? Chips and dips,
In our world, it's the little trips.

No need for maps, or global quests,
We live our best in comfy vests.
For every step, a joyful cheer,
In every corner, we persevere.

So follow me, let's wander free,
In pure confusion, there's glee, you see?
A compass lost, but never fear,
We'll find our way, with snacks and beer.

The Freedom in Unwritten Chapters

Blank pages lie, oh what a treat,
Adventure waits beneath our feet.
No rules to bind, no scripts to write,
We dance in chaos, pure delight.

Who needs a map on this wild ride?
We'll laugh and jiggle, side by side.
With each wrong turn, a tale to weave,
In this grand mess, we'll still believe.

A sprinkle of chaos, a dash of fun,
The plot thickens as we run.
With every page we choose to skip,
We raise our mugs, and take a sip.

The best stories start with a laugh,
Forget the cut scenes, embrace the gaff.
No end in sight, just joy in the chase,
We'll write our tales at our own pace.

Celebrating the Quiet Moments

In the stillness, chaos makes a scene,
Counting dust bunnies, oh what a dream!
With a giggle at life's little quirks,
We find joy lurking in oddworks.

Moments pass, like clouds in the sky,
With smiles that whisper, and jokes that fly.
Unexpected giggles, tickle the soul,
In the quiet chaos, we become whole.

Subtle joys, like socks that don't match,
Brewing good tea while we sit and hatch.
The moments we share, the laughs that we keep,
In every silence, something to reap.

So raise a toast to the day's little tasks,
In the tiniest pleasures, humor unmasked.
We dance to the rhythm of unscripted grace,
Finding the magic in life's holding space.

When Certainty Wears Thin

Certainty's caper starts to fray,
Life's a circus; come join the play!
With shadows of doubt creeping near,
We'll laugh out loud, dismissing fear.

When plans collapse like houses of cards,
We'll juggle dreams and laugh at the shards.
With every slip, we find our tone,
In the beautiful mess, we aren't alone.

Riding on whims like a carnival ride,
We toss expectations, slinging them wide.
The joy in the mishaps, it's truly sublime,
In the game of life, let's dare to rhyme.

So let's sip on chaos, laughing away,
Wandering paths that are free from cliché.
In the ebb and flow, we find our song,
When certainty falters, we still belong.

Sipping Tea with Uncertainty

With a teacup clutched, we sit and sip,
Tasting the whims of this wild trip.
Uncertainty's flavor, a dash of zest,
In every drop, we find our rest.

Like leaves swirling in a pot of brew,
Our thoughts drift past, both old and new.
With laughter bubbling, we spill our dreams,
In this quirky dance, nothing's as it seems.

Sugar and spice, forget the rulebook,
With every sip, we take a look.
At life's little pranks, we giggle and cheer,
Finding the fun in what's unclear.

So here's to the brews in life's crazy cup,
We'll laugh at the waves, and drink it all up.
With uncertainty's charm as our silly muse,
In every sip, the joy we choose.

Embracing Aimless Wandering

Lost in the aisles of the grocery store,
My cart holds snacks I truly adore.
Maps and plans? I don't need that fluff,
Spontaneity is just way more fun stuff.

Chasing dreams, they say, brings you cheer,
But I'd rather chase down a cold root beer.
Who needs a guide for a whimsical quest?
With chips in my hand, I feel truly blessed.

The Silence of Unfulfilled Ambitions

Ambitions shout loud, like a toddler's toy,
But I prefer naps and a couch's soft joy.
Goals can be tricky, a tangled old mess,
I'll just binge-watch shows; it's a real success.

Some plan for futures that sparkle and gleam,
While I settle for lunch and a lazy day dream.
Whispers of "grow up!" echo and fade,
In the kingdom of naps, I'm an esteemed trade.

Revelry in Routine

Every morning I wake, with coffee in hand,
And marvel at toast—such a magical land!
Routine is a dance, oh, what a delight,
Why reach for the stars when breakfast's in sight?

Shiny notebooks and planners galore,
But I'd rather scribble on a napkin, I swore.
Step by step, I take life in stride,
With a scone in the basket, I'm joyful inside.

A Journey Without a Map

Maps lead to places, but I'm not convinced,
I'll just wander around, feeling quite ginned.
Winding paths and a picnic in hand,
Every bend holds a mystery, oh so grand!

Some seek the summit, the peak of a hill,
But I'll just stroll slowly, enjoying the thrill.
With whims and tickles in every direction,
The best detours bring laughter and connection.

A Journey Without a Final Destination

Wanderers we roam, with no map in hand,
In search of meaning we can barely understand.
Eating snacks on the road, our worries tossed,
Counting silly moments, forget the cost.

A traveler's tale with no end in sight,
We laugh at the stars, in the velvet night.
With flip-flops on feet, we dance through the muck,
Who needs a purpose? We're just out of luck!

We stumble and trip over thoughts, quite absurd,
Like chasing a butterfly, as it's never heard.
Taking selfies with clouds, what a splendid view,
As goals keep eluding, we just giggle anew!

So here's to the journey, the joy in the ride,
With no final destination, let's enjoy the tide.
In this whimsical chase, we find our delight,
Here's laughing at traffic while missing the flight!

Finding Peace in the Unraveled Threads.

In knitting pursuit, I lost all the yarn,
My sweater's a poncho; I'm not one to scorn.
With each tangled stitch, I chuckle and sigh,
Perfection's for robots, I'm just too spry!

Embracing the frays that dangle and tease,
I wear mismatched socks with the greatest of ease.
The fabric of life, it unravels for fun,
Why chase after gold when I've already won?

Needle in hand, I'm a seamstress of cheer,
Through knots and loops, my path becomes clear.
In the mess of the thread, a pattern appears,
It's all about laughter, not worthiness fears!

So onward I go, with my rogue ball of twine,
To craft out a joy that's simply divine.
In the quilt of existence, imperfectly sewn,
I find all the peace that I've ever known!

Whispers of Worthlessness

In the echoes of thoughts, my doubts softly croon,
Like socks missing pairs, they float like a tune.
Feeling all special in my not-so-fine mind,
Embracing the chaos, no path left behind.

Whispers of worthlessness, they buzz in my head,
Like leftover pizza, they just won't be fed.
I laugh at their nonsense, let them waltz on by,
With jokes about failures, I'll just let out a sigh.

In a dance of confusion, I'm twirling about,
Wearing a crown made of the things I doubt.
With confetti of questions, I throw my hands high,
Who needs validation? I'm the fanciest guy!

The echoes may linger, but here's what I'll do,
I'll shake off their whispers, and I'll still pull through.
For in every misstep, there's laughter and cheer,
In the land of the lost, I'm the one that they hear!

Chasing Shadows of Significance

In a world where shadows stretch long on the ground,
I chase after nonsense, and laughter is found.
With a magnifying glass, I search for my fate,
But the universe chuckles, says I'm just late.

These shadows of meaning, they play hard to get,
I swipe at their edges, but no net has been set.
They giggle and flutter, like butterflies' flight,
Why bother with answers? Just dance through the night!

Oh! Deep thoughts and pursuits that seem far away,
I'll laugh with my coffee, on a bright sunny day.
With whimsy my compass, I'll stroll through the mock,
Each shadow worth chasing, hand in hand with the clock.

So here's to the wander, the seeker inside,
With shadows to chase, there's no need to hide.
Let's frolic through musings that don't make a fuss,
In this chase for significance—we can all just combust!

Scribbles on a Blank Canvas

With colors splashed like morning sun,
The artist laughs, 'This looks like fun!'
A line that's crooked, a dot that's round,
Who needs a plan when joy's abound?

A splash of red, a dash of blue,
"Abstract?" I think, "What does that do?"
A squiggly line, a playful caper,
Who knew mistakes could be such paper?

A canvas bare, yet full of glee,
My cat walks through—oh, what a spree!
The masterpiece? Just my cat's big paw,
Art's just a laugh, and that's the law!

So here I dance with colors bright,
In this crazy mess, it feels just right.
No need for meaning or a grand career,
I'll paint my joy, my path's quite clear!

The Beauty of Banal Moments

A toast to crumbs on kitchen floors,
Life's greatest triumph? Finding doors!
The coffee's cold, the toast is burnt,
Yet laughter, oh, that's what I've yearned!

Watching paint dry, a thrilling game,
Who knew tedium could earn you fame?
Each tick of the clock, a curious friend,
In stillness, joy starts to blend.

The dog's chasing shadows, what a sight,
While I contemplate my next big bite.
Chores like these are profound, you see,
In mundanity, I find the key!

So revel in moments that seem quite bland,
Like picking daisies from soft, warm sand.
In the whirl of chaos and daily grind,
The laughter's there, if you seek to find!

Unpacking the Burden of Beliefs

In the attic of thoughts, so dusty and old,
I find belief bags, some tarnished with mold.
Each one I lift, I shake and I peer,
Some might be treasures; others, I fear!

A box marked 'Success,' quite heavy indeed,
But wait, it's just receipts for things I don't need.
Another with dreams, all stuffed to the very
Then I found a sock—now isn't that merry?

The box of regrets? It can't fit my smile,
I'll close it up tight; it won't stay a while.
No need for burdens or hefty weights,
Let's replace them with chocolate and open gates!

So toss out the baggage, the weights full of strife,
Unpack the good, let's enjoy this life.
For belief's just a game, a bit of disguise,
I'll choose fun and laughter as my prize!

Contentment in Chaos

Amidst the clutter, I sip my tea,
Oh what a mess! But it's home to me.
Sock on the ceiling, a shoe in the fridge,
Finding those silly things makes me smidge!

The cat thinks chaos is just a grand game,
While I question if I'm really the same.
But life's little quirks are sweet and divine,
In the whirlwind of madness, my joy starts to shine!

A tangle of wires, a puzzle unsolved,
Yet within the chaos, I've found I've evolved.
I embrace the absurd, it tickles my heart,
In this messy play, I'm a master of art!

So bring on the chaos, I'll dance with the tide,
In this whirlwind of laughter, let joy be my guide.
For in every calamity, a giggle's concealed,
Life's chaos, my canvas; watch the joy be revealed!

The Joy of Ordinary Days

Woke up to socks that don't match,
Made coffee that tasted like ash.
Yet here I sit, no grand design,
Just a donut and a slice of time.

Chasing cats instead of my dreams,
Finding humor in fading beams.
Living loud in mundane ways,
Oh, the joy of ordinary days!

Flickering Flames of Unfulfilled Aspirations

My goals are like burnt toast, you see,
Charred hopes staring back at me.
I wanted to zigzag through life's grand dance,
But tripped over my own last chance.

Candles flicker, yet I stay bold,
Embracing stories left untold.
In quirky ways, I find my cheer,
As I chase down every weird frontier.

When Tomorrow Becomes Yesterday

Plan all I want, it slips away,
Like ice cream on a sunny day.
Tomorrow puffs its chest so loud,
Yet here I am, lost in the crowd.

What was the plan? I can't recall,
Thoughts scatter like leaves in the fall.
Yesterday's worries? What a thrill!
Let's dance on whims and misfit will!

Wandering Souls in Search of Nothing

With shoes untied and minds askew,
We roam the world, it's what we do.
Chasing shadows, we find delight,
In empty rooms and starry nights.

Here's to the lost in hilarious quests,
Seeking treasures in silly tests.
Finding joy in the lack of a track,
Wandering souls never look back.

Moments That Go Unnoticed

The cat naps while the kettle hums,
Forgotten socks create their own drums.
A toast to crumbs on the dining room floor,
Happiness found in the smallest of lore.

A sneeze that echoes in the crowded hall,
A surprise when my pencil decided to fall.
In the shade of a tree, squirrels play tag,
While I sit sipping tea from a rusty old rag.

Birds tweet gossip with a cheeky delight,
As I trip on a rug in the soft morning light.
Life's odd little quirks, they come and then go,
Unnoticed moments that steal the show.

So here's to the things that barely amuse,
Like the way my dog gives his tail a big cruise.
In the dance of the mundane, there lies a bright cheer,
Let's laugh at the moments, for they vanish, my dear.

Reflections in a Still Pool

In a puddle, I glimpse my own silly face,
Making the moment a chaotic race.
The duck quacks back, it's an odd little game,
While I ponder the meaning of fame and my name.

The trees whisper secrets, but I cannot hear,
Perhaps they're just chatting about the next deer.
I wave at the clouds, they float by with glee,
As I dodge around pigeons who laugh at me.

Looking for wisdom, I found a goldfish,
Swam in circles, with quite a good wish.
What's the grand scheme, should I even care?
The ripples in water just dance with my hair.

So splash about, ponder the trivial chase,
For the dance of the day is a silly embrace.
In the quiet reflections of what seems so bleak,
Laughter's the answer, not some lofty peak.

A Joyful Noise in a Silent World

The noise of my toaster is music divine,
As burnt edges toast, no grand sign of a shrine.
My sock puppet sings in a bright, silly tone,
A duet with dust bunnies, never alone.

The fridge hums a lullaby, cold and sincere,
While my cat starts a symphony, loud and unclear.
Mismatched spoons gather, like friends for a chat,
Creating a ruckus with a fanciful pat.

A spatula joins in, with a clatter and clang,
While the old clock just ticks, with a well-timed twang.
In a world quietapped by the weight of demands,
The joy's in the chaos, and not in the plans.

So let's make a racket, embrace the absurd,
With laughter and music, let's not be deterred.
For in silly moments, we find a bright spark,
A joyful noise ignites even the dark.

The Weight of Wishing

I tossed a coin in the fountain of dreams,
But it just splashed water, that's not what it seems.
With every small wish, I weighed down my heart,
Will the universe care? It's a whimsical art.

Balloons float high, yet I trip on the ground,
As greatness gives chase, it's nowhere to be found.
I scribble my desires on the back of my hand,
Only to find they're as light as fine sand.

A wish for a sandwich, or maybe for gold,
Turns into a quick snooze, if truth be told.
In the weight of wishing, I find no distress,
For simplicity's charm is the true, bold finesse.

So wish me good luck with my luckless parade,
May my queries be curious and never dismayed.
For what's worth desiring isn't much worth the flight,
Let's toast to the absurdities that bring us delight!

Dreams That Once Sparkled Dimmed

Once I aimed for glittering heights,
Now I nap through the cosmic flights.
My goals tossed aside like old socks,
Chasing joy from my backyard box.

The stars I wished upon, long gone,
Just like that snack I thought was on.
I trade ambition for comfy shoes,
It's a riot, not just a ruse.

Who knew the thrill was in the cheese?
Or snuggled deep among the trees?
With every nap, my dreams refute,
And I snack again—oh sweet pursuit!

Here's to laughter in this plight,
Find me smiling, day or night.
Though sparkles fade, we'll still embrace,
A life of joy, not just a race.

The Weight of Expectations Unraveled

Everyone's got a grand design,
But my plan's to just recline.
Tied to trends like wayward kites,
I prefer my couch and bites.

They say I should have perfect dreams,
But all I want are whipped cream streams.
Balancing pressures, I stumble and spill,
Found joy in chaos, and that's my thrill.

With each burden, I toss away,
Creating my own bright disarray.
The weight of life? Give me a break!
I'll take a nap instead of fate.

So here's to treasures in messy fights,
Like chips and salsa on stormy nights.
Abandoning anchors so tight and grim,
An unplanned voyage, let the fun begin!

Searching for Stars in a Gloomy Sky

On cloudy days, I squint and stare,
With high hopes and mismatched pair.
But if the stars play hard to find,
I'll just chase snacks, oh how refined!

The forecast says no cosmic show,
So I'll create my own glow.
With each chips crunch, the stars align,
And my soda pop is simply divine.

A gloomy sky becomes a feast,
For silly dreams that never ceased.
Though constellations are stuck in fright,
I'll laugh 'til morning, holding tight.

In simple moments, I find the spark,
An inner glow, a loving lark.
Who needs the stars to have some fun,
As long as I can laugh—I've won!

Freedom in Uncertainty

What is a plan? What's that supposed to mean?
I'll just wing it, fresh and keen!
With a compass stuck to my shoelace,
I stumble forward—what a chase!

The thrill of 'maybe' is all I crave,
Ditching the map, I choose to rave.
No need for order in this dance,
We'll figure it out—might as well prance!

Embracing chaos, my thoughts unwind,
With random snacks, each day's defined.
In this soup of whimsy and wit,
I laugh and tumble, I'm loving it!

The joy of life is what we create,
So bring on herbs, we're feeling great!
No need for answers while we jest,
In this kooky venture, I'm truly blessed!

The Tapestry of Everyday Tales

Woke up in my fuzzy socks,
And tripped over the dog's nice box.
Coffee spilled, I can't complain,
It's my new morning routine, plain!

Forgot my wallet at the mall,
But found a thirty in the hall.
Life's too short for grand design,
Let's just see what we can find.

Random socks and mismatched shoes,
I'm rocking all the crazy hues.
With every step, I laugh and grin,
Worrying 'bout the purpose? Nah, we win!

Counting dust bunnies, they do dance,
In this chaotic life, I glance.
The answer's simpler than we thought,
Just enjoy the random that we've got!

Revelations from the Sidelines

Why chase dreams like a racing car,
When couch surfing feels like a star?
Remote in hand, I watch it all,
Like a king upon my fluffy thrall.

Success? Just a pizza slice,
Topped with cheese and extra spice.
With each bite, I feel so grand,
Kings of frozen, we make our stand.

Glimpses of wisdom from sitcom laughs,
Finding joy in everyday gaffes.
Who needs fate when you've got chips?
And soda bubbles 'long with quips?

The world rushes, but I just pause,
To savor snacks and give applause.
Life's tricky, but I've made my peace,
By simply enjoying—let worries cease!

The Blessing of Nearby Sunsets

No need to chase the distant sun,
When every sunset's full of fun!
I plop on grass, a blanket spread,
And watch those colors dance instead.

Forget the worries that we scheme,
Just pop some corn and share a dream.
Nature's canvas, free for all,
No fancy brushes, just a ball!

As clouds drift by, my snack in hand,
I plot my stay on this soft land.
An artist's heart, but in a chair,
With warm hues cradled in the air.

It's perfect here, with laughter loud,
Seeking sunsets, not the crowd.
A life well-spent is made of play,
In colors that just fade away!

Observations from the Ordinary

Watching pigeons strut their stuff,
While I sit here, feeling tough.
They coo and hop, like little kings,
What a life that simple brings!

Why fret about the grand designs,
When bread crumbs are the best of signs?
The little joys, they come in flocks,
Like friendship shared on park-side rocks.

Tripping over life's bizarre ways,
Finding magic in mundane days.
A sock that's lost, a book that's bent,
Or coffee made—such joy, I meant!

So take a fast-paced world and slow,
Appreciate the antics we all know.
In ordinary things, we reign supreme,
And there's humor tucked in every dream!

Solace in the Unadorned

In a world of grand designs,
I choose my cereal, no wine.
A life of simple, silly fun,
Where chores are less and naps are won.

My plants are fake, they don't need care,
No watering can, just vacant stare.
I garden with plastic, you can't tell—
Sunshine and dirt? Oh, what the hell!

I laugh at woes that come my way,
Why fret when socks have gone astray?
Embrace the silly, let it fly,
Who needs a map? Just try to fly!

So let us dance, ignore the frown,
With every slip, we'll spin around.
For joy's a game that's meant to play,
Without a goal—just here today.

The Beauty of Barely There

An empty plate is my delight,
No fancy dish, just appetite!
When guests arrive, it's pizza night,
Who needs a roast, if it's done right?

My goals are vague, much like my hair,
Wandering round without a care.
A nap, a snack, repeat the cycle,
Chasing dreams? Nah, I'll ride a tricycle.

I watch the clouds, they float and stall,
All meanings lost, I heed their call.
Life's best when it skims the surface,
Like a dime store book with no purpose.

So toast to fun in every fluke,
No need for vows or solemn Duke.
Let laughter be my only creed,
In this less-traveled path, I lead.

Musing on the Meaningless

In this circus of the odd and strange,
Where nothing stays and things can change,
I ponder meanings lost in air,
While scoffing at the world's despair.

A coffee spills, I laugh it off,
No grand plans, just playful scoff.
My to-do list? Just doodles and dreams,
Feeling great in these silly themes.

Call it chaos, call it flair,
I collect moments lying bare.
As purpose drips like melting ice,
I'll take a shot at rolling dice.

So let's embrace this charming mess,
With giggles hiding all the stress.
For in this dance, we find our song,
No need for right, just sing along.

The Art of Living for Laughter

Tickling funny bones each day,
With laughter leading the way.
A giggle here, a snort right there,
Life's a joke we all can share.

Why ponder deep when we can jest?
Chasing joy is simply the best.
In silly hats and pudgy shoes,
We find the laugh that we can use.

Forget the weight of heavy frowns,
Just toss 'em out, and spin around.
With puns and jests, we live with glee,
It's all a game, just let it be.

So dance a dance of pure delight,
In cosmic chaos, shine so bright.
To laugh is art; we are the jest,
Adventures found in every quest.

Finding Freedom in the Ordinary

A cup of coffee spills its cheer,
As socks collide, oh dear, oh dear!
In mundane tasks, we often find,
A giggle lurking, so unconfined.

The shopping list, a thrilling mess,
A misstep here, a shoe to press.
Who knew that chaos could inspire,
To laugh at life and never tire?

Unfolding laundry like a game,
With each lost sock, we'll cheer the name!
For in the wash of daily grind,
We find the sparkle, so well-defined.

Embrace the normal, laugh it loud,
Find joy within the bustling crowd.
The ordinary sings with funny notes,
Life's simple groove, that's how it floats.

The Fallacy of a Grand Plan

Maps and schematics can be a bore,
When spontaneity opens a door.
With twists and turns, the route is ours,
Adventure blooms like summer flowers.

Who needs a plan when we can play?
Surprises await on any old day.
Let plans fall through like soggy bread,
Reveal the joys of paths instead.

Chasing dreams? That just sounds fine,
But not if that means losing time.
Let's paddle boats, not draft a diagram,
Just follow whimsy like the gentle ram!

In a cosmic joke, we'll simply float,
With laughter riding on a boat.
Raise a toast to every twist and bend,
The grand design? Just laugh and blend.

Embracing the Mundane

Whisking eggs and stirring stew,
What joy is found in daily brew!
A scrape, a splatter, just let it go,
In mess and chaos, laughter flows.

Dirt on shoes and crumbs on floors,
Every hiccup opens doors.
Tripping over shoes we tossed,
In every fall, we gain, not lost.

A ringing phone, a cat that meows,
In every sound, a chuckle bows.
With chores that hum a silly tune,
The mundane waltzes under the moon.

Let's celebrate the average day,
For in its charm, we laugh and play.
With every hiccup, life's parade,
We find the joy; we're unafraid.

The Poetry of Not Knowing

I woke up today, no grand plan in sight,
Coffee in hand, my future feels light.
Maybe I'll nap or binge on TV,
Who needs a goal? Just let it be free.

I tried to be wise, but that turned out wrong,
The mysteries of life are a silly old song.
I dance with my socks in the middle of the street,
Nothing like laughter to make my day sweet.

With maps that are blurry and charts all unclear,
I wander through moments, embracing the cheer.
Why chase a rainbow when the sun's shining high?
I'll paint my own clouds, let the colors fly.

So I'll celebrate chaos, an unscripted spree,
Sipping my coffee, just chuckling with glee.
Each clueless adventure brings forth a new gem,
In the art of just living, I'm my own zen.

Constellations Beyond Ambition

The stars shine bright, but I lost my way,
Chasing the moon, but it led me astray.
I tried to reach fortune, but slipped on a pear,
Now I just stargaze from my comfy chair.

Ambition is great, or so they say loud,
But I find true joy just kicking around.
With snacks in my pouch and a drink in my hand,
I'm the king of pajama, the ruler of sand.

So while others rush, I stroll through the haze,
In the parade of the goofy, I'll forever amaze.
If dreams can be silly, then let them unfold,
For laughter's the currency worth more than gold.

In a galaxy filled with plans set to fail,
I'll opt for a joke, my own merry trail.
There's meaning in nonsense, or so I believe,
In the stars of each chuckle, I find my reprieve.

Where the Heart Roams Free

I chased my ambitions, but they ran away,
Now my heart roams wild, like a dog gone astray.
I'll wander the fields, with a smile and a skip,
Who needs a destination? Just let it rip!

With shoes untied and a hat on askew,
I prance through the meadows, enjoying the view.
The purpose is tricky, let's give it a twist,
For joy is the treasure that can't be missed.

Each path that I take is a party for one,
Dancing with daisies, soaking up sun.
Forget about futures, they'll come like a breeze,
With snacks in my pocket, I'm truly at ease.

Amongst the wildflowers, I laugh and I play,
No maps or compasses will get in my way.
For a heart that is free is the best way to roam,
In the garden of giggles, I've found my true home.

A Symphony of Wistful Whispers

The symphony plays on, with a note out of tune,
Each whim a crescendo, beneath the full moon.
I twirl with the melodies, lost in the sound,
Every laugh is a lyric, joyfully found.

In the orchestra chaos, I can hear life sing,
Who needs a conductor when fun's the true king?
With pops and with cracks, we shall dance through the night,
For silly is sacred, and wrong feels so right.

As moments collide like a band playing loud,
I'll join in the chorus, be silly, be proud.
A wink and a nudge, take a bow if you dare,
For the funny and weird make a wonderful pair.

So let's laugh with abandon, let our spirits be bold,
In the whispers of whimsy, true treasures unfold.
A life filled with giggles, my favorite refrain,
In this symphony waltz, there's nothing to gain.

Navigating Through Foggy Expectations

In a world so bright, at times quite blurry,
I sail my ship, but oh so slurry.
The maps I follow, all smudged with doubt,
Each turn I take, I'm still left out.

Paddling through tides of 'should' and 'must',
I can't recall, so I just trust.
With foggy views, my compass spins,
I giggle softly at all my sins.

Chasing dreams wrapped up in haze,
Wandering through life's comical maze.
What's the rush? The clock's a tease,
So I'll just nap beneath the trees.

The Serenity of Being Unremarkable

Oh, blissful calm, no need to shine,
Just blending in, that suits me fine.
With not a headline, nor grand parade,
I'm in the crowd, a quiet shade.

Life's not a race, it's a leisurely walk,
Where small talk's gold and no one mocks.
In mediocrity, I find delight,
As others stress about their flight.

No Oscar nods, no Nobel prize,
Just evening chats 'neath amber skies.
Serenity blooms when one stays small,
The art of nothing is the best of all.

Finding Bliss in Forgetfulness

In the realm of slip and slide,
I lose my keys, they run to hide.
Forgotten names and faces blend,
Yet in this mess, my joy won't end.

What was the plan? Who am I now?
Chaos reigns, yet I take a bow.
For bliss is found in little things,
Like yesterday's unexpected flings.

Out of the blue, I laugh and grin,
For what's a day without some spin?
With all my thoughts a jigsaw mix,
I celebrate each blissful fix.

Echoes of Entropy

With every step, a playful dance,
Chaos whispers, 'Take a chance!'
In disarray, there's pure delight,
Moments blur and take to flight.

Each sock misplaced, a riddle bent,
Lost in joy, time's president.
Like socks and spoons that go astray,
I forge my path in charming dismay.

Embrace the mess, let laughter reign,
For what's a life that's tight and plain?
Echoing giggles in every turn,
In entropy's arms, it's bliss I yearn.

www.ingramcontent.com/pod-product-compliance
Lightning Source LLC
Chambersburg PA
CBHW072145200426
43209CB00051B/593